MARCIA

MARCIA:
Poems From The Heart

Marcia M. Harvey

Copyright © 1996, 2011 by Marcia M. Harvey.

ISBN:　　　　Softcover　　　　　　978-1-4628-5387-8
　　　　　　 Ebook　　　　　　　　978-1-4628-5388-5

All rights reserved. No part of this book may be reproduced or transmitted in any form or by any means, electronic or mechanical, including photocopying, recording, or by any information storage and retrieval system, without permission in writing from the copyright owner.

This book was printed in the United States of America.

To order additional copies of this book, contact:
Xlibris Corporation
1-888-795-4274
www.Xlibris.com
Orders@Xlibris.com
95911

Dedication

This book is dedicated to my Lord and Savior, Jesus Christ, who is my sustainer. Without you, Jesus, I would not be the woman of God I am today proclaiming Your name with the confidence and boldness that I do. You suffered and died so that I could live in the power and authority of Your resurrection. You delivered me, transformed me, rebuilt me, protected me and covered me so that I may be used by You for Your greater purpose. God I thank you for choosing me. Your unconditional love is immeasurable and will never be understood by the human mind . . .

Thank you to my friends and amazing family for believing in me (a special thank you to Candace for helping me finish putting this book together and to Angie for giving me the resources to do it). Dad, Mom, John, Dana, Andrew, Alan and Andrea, your prayers, love, and encouragement have helped birth this 23 year old vision. I appreciate your support and obedience to the Holy Spirit. Thank you to my children who have been my light through some dark tunnels. I love you boys!

Lastly, I am grateful for the seasons of my life and the people associated with them. I am who I am because of every laugh, cry, heartache, love, heartbreak, betrayal, mistake, success, failure, loss and gain. Today I stand victorious, in Christ Jesus; regardless of the trials and tribulations . . . it all works for my good!

Psalm 96:3-4 Publish his glorious deeds among the nations. Tell everyone about the amazing things he does. Great is the LORD! He is most worthy of praise! (NLT)

CONTENTS

PAST

- Parents 13
- Memories 14
- Life 15
- War of the Roses 16
- Happy Days 17
- Moving On 18
- Love Dreams 19
- Someone Special 20
- Kisses in the Night 21
- Goodbye 22
- My Future 23
- Tears of Yesterday 24
- Why Me? 25

PRESENT

- The Broken-Hearted One ... 29
- A New Beginning 30
- The Forgotten One 31
- The Unknown 32
- To Struggle 33
- Deadly Stalker 34
- Wishing 35
- Bewildered 36
- Misled 37
- Love at First Sight 38
- For the Love of Her 39
- Can't Let Go 40
- Home 41
- Higher Ground 42
- Betrayed 43
- My Heart Still Yearns 44
- So Smooth 45
- Why? 46

FUTURE

- Feeling the Unknown 49
- My Sweet Love 50
- Dream Man......................... 51
- Mood of the Day................ 52
- Just To 53
- Test of Time 54
- I Laugh 55
- Lips of Fire 56
- Opportunity Knocks........... 57
- Lost Love............................. 58
- How Can Life...................... 59
- Three Falls 60
- A Way Out 61
- Shades of Black.................. 62
- Black is 63
- The Sun Still Shines............ 64
- Friend?................................. 65

PAST

PARENTS

P*eople who have a family in which they keep strong;*
A*lways by our side when we're right and when we're wrong.*
R*eady to love in the time of need;*
E*ager to face trials in which they lead, us*
N*ever to lose faith, it's from them we feed.*
T*hanking you for all the things you two have ever done;*
S*aying and hoping we will always be, together as one.*

Memories

You and I together forever;
Being with you I hoped to endeavor.

Having love quarrels, swinging love taps;
Kissing and hugging, taking little naps.

Sharing our thoughts or innermost feelings;
Hoping we would make a precious human being.

We were like bees at a hive;
Without one another we couldn't survive.

But things have changed, we've both moved on;
We're falling apart and I hope not for long.

I will never forget you, for my heart you were the keys;
And I hope we never let go of these memories.

Life

Days and nights of pain and heartache;
Like a nightmare which I cannot awake.

Trapped in life, a living hell;
Stuck in jail or living cell.

Struggling to get out, trying to escape;
Similar to a child who has been raped.

A horror which she has to live;
Scarred for life, with nothing to give.

Leading to suffering and strength taken away;
Trailing behind as a lost stray.

All I do now is wonder and stare;
Praying for support and tender-loving care!!!!!

War of the Roses

The struggle between two loves is tearing me apart;
I'm so confused with nothing to do, it's breaking my heart.

I can't help but to want the past to be part of the present;
But I don't want my life to be the way that it went.

I'm stuck in a time zone, lost in time;
I can't decide which love to call mine.

Knowing I'll go back to what it was before;
I want to move on; I can't weep for him anymore.

I need to come back to life and reality;
Because I'm not living in a dream or fantasy.

Reminiscing of the times we used to talk;
Playing silly games and taking little walks.

The arguments, lies, and shedding of tears;
Tore us apart instead of keeping us near.

Oh the dreams I have in which I fear;
If only my cries were for someone to hear . . .

Happy Days

The worst is over, the best is yet to come;
Happy days are here and then some.

No more depression or crying at night;
Darkness has passed, in comes the light.

New head on your shoulders, smile on your face;
On the right track, leading the race.

He touched your heart and saw you through;
Without Him, there's nothing you can do.

When times were rough and no one was there;
It was God that carried you, He was there.

It's time to praise and thank Him for what He's done;
Because if it wasn't for Him, there would be none.

Hallelujah, thank the Lord in so many ways;
We have finally come to our Happy Days.

Moving On

*Boasting with euphoria, feeling so good inside;
I think it's 'cause I'm over him, it's something I can't hide.*

*The Lord has put joy in my heart;
A feeling I should have had from the start.*

*There is so much happiness I feel I will explode;
I'm finally on the right track and on the golden road.*

*I've found someone new who seems really sweet;
He gives me a love that can't be beat.*

*Cute as a button, smart as an owl;
It's my turn now, no need to throw in the towel.*

*I'm a queen on top of the world;
No more foolishness in which I had curled.*

*The past is in the past, the future is to come;
I'm taking a new approach, I have to change some.*

*Little boys' games will now be banned;
I'm looking for TLC found in a real man!*

Love Dreams

*Time and time again I sit and wonder,
what has happened to me, is my life going under?*

*When we were together I was his only one,
but when we were apart he was always on the run.*

*I was loyal to him and for everything I've done,
what thanks do I get . . . NONE!*

*Playing the role like I was his forever, his only one I hoped to endeavor.
So when was it true that I was really his . . . NEVER!
It's o.k. 'cause he'll suffer.*

*Imagining the way I wanted it to seem,
caught up in this crazy thing called Love Dreams.
Not knowing reality or his schemes,
dazing about these crazy Love Dreams.*

*Caught in a love trap with nowhere to hide,
on my own with no man by my side.
Just a devious boy who wants a quick joy ride.
Used again, played like cards;
I never can tell, it's always too hard.*

*Wondering if I'll ever get on the right track,
hoping if I'll change and never look back.
Because if I don't then I'll be like a tack in a knapsack,
stuck on a rack for good and that's whack.
No more can I lack, he has to hit the road Jack.*

*Imagining the way I wanted it to seem,
caught up in this crazy thing called Love Dreams.
Not knowing reality or his schemes,
dazing about these crazy Love Dreams.*

*Tired of getting hurt, I have to be strong.
I have to move on this can't last for long,
and to you I want to dedicate this song!!!!!!*

Someone Special

You came into my life now everything's change;
I was in control but now my life is rearranged.

I can't handle what I do, or how I feel inside;
I try to hold it in but it's something I can't hide.

The way you look at me and hold me in your arms;
You seem to be a gentleman and can't mean any harm.

Even though you claim to be wild and kind of tough;
To me you are sweet and caring and not really that rough.

Very cute and funny too;
There's an everlasting love from me to you.

Romantic, loving, and also kind;
I hope you're never looking for another girl to find.

Other guys mean nothing to me, it's you in which I'd nestle;
Never burdening you or hurting you because you're someone special!

Kisses in the Night

As I go to sleep, he kisses me goodnight;
Then I dream a nightmare and awake in fright.

Dreaming everlasting love we will find;
Then becoming a monster, keeping us bind.

His kisses in the night made me bear;
The upcoming nightmares which I dared.

But no more kisses comfort my depression;
The dreams are now a day by day obsession.

He's no longer here in my possession;
Which digresses my goals and life's progression.

He kissed me in the night to prepare me for the next day;
To be aware of his love and never stray.

"I believed that circles never end, I guess it's still true;
We were never in a circle, forever wasn't meant for me and you!"

Goodbye

Saying goodbye is hard to do;
I'd never thought it would happen between us two.
Whatever happened to, "I'll never let you go!"
Was it how you felt or part of your game, I really need to know!?
I'm going to miss your kisses in the night;
The polishing of my toes and even our fights.
My heart is broken again; do you realize you used me?
And that poor excuse of love, you knew that you would lose me.
You had it all figured out, your plan was quite a task;
You got what you wanted; there was no need to ask.
I fell into your trap and I'm sorry that I did;
Our worlds could never bind; you're a greedy little kid.
I hope that you grow up and change your mind;
Sex is NOT needed to complete a relationship,
Other ways you must find.
You really don't love me, never did and never will;
You think sex is love because your heart it fills.
But it's not your heart that yearns, it's your emotions,
You're not supposed to give into them, you see the commotion;
Caused between you and also someone dear;
Now you're confused, your car is out of gear.
Sure, go back to your "old ways," run away from the problem;
You won't get very far, you need to solve them.
Whether you believe it or not, allow God to see you through;
He'll turn your life around and make your heart brand new.
So you'll be able to love the right way, not the wrong;
The way you've wanted to love and be loved for so long.
When you met me, you fell into more than meets the eye;
But as for yesterday, it's time to say goodbye!!!!!!!!!!

My Future

*My future holds a vast of experiences I hope you are in,
sharing my every thought and dream.
Beginning a life together lasting a lifetime.
We shall love with an Agape love, as God has loved us;
Never deserting one another no matter the steep or consequence.
Respecting one another as I, your queen, and you, my king.
Sheltered by God's love, we shall never perish but fall at sin,
like a teardrop from one's eye.
Overcoming our desires until the time is right to be one.
Tending to your every need, and you to mine;
"We shall be patient and kind to one another; never jealous or
boastful, never arrogant or rude, nor insist in our own way, and THEN,
our love shall rejoice in the right and not the wrong."
In unity, we can accomplish anything our hearts desire,
even the hardest task will blow by like a gentle breeze.
I hope you are ready to handle what you're getting into, for even the
eager heart is not prepared to settle beyond the surface of the flesh!
Are you? . . .*

Tears of Yesterday

*As I go to sleep, I wonder about you and me together.
I fantasize of what it would be like; hand and hand strolling down the riverside banks at sunset.
But in the midst of it, my mind seems to deter to the scene of "Memory Lane".
Possessed by the terrors of my past, I can't reach for the future.
The wrath of present days has me wrapped in fear of reliving the past.
Suffering again and again,
he has me trapped like a spider's prey caught in its web.
I can't escape the fire.
The harder I try to break free, the more I am surrounded by the flames.
Entangled in my emotions and convictions,
I'm being stretched out by two extremes.
Swallowed by yesterday, refuge is far from near.
But all is well; Grace is just around the corner . . .
If only I could reach it!*

Why Me?

As I gaze into the stars, "Alpha, I wonder, why me?"
Being tortured by this world, I'm blind and need to see.

Principalities no longer rule in this hell of hells;
Evil has conquered good yet He says all is well.

Buildings have collapsed, the storm is on the rise;
I am in the midst, defeat has overcome my eyes.

Ice could not last in hell, nor I in this place;
I can't go on any longer, let me forfeit the race.

I want to go Home, surrounded by Glory I shall stand;
I will sing with the angels and walk with the Omega hand in hand.

PRESENT

The Broken-Hearted One

*Under that cute little smile lies a bruised soul.
Your spirit no longer sings with the angels of Heaven for you have been disowned by a necessity that you thought you'd have forever.
Don't give up; Grace is just around the corner.
Though you feel life is over, it has just begun.
God will bring you through and you shall build character by this.
Keep smiling broken-hearted one, your smile will soon be real;
For when one is lost another is gained and is more precious that the first.
Strive to reach your goal to love and be loved again, the right way, and you shall succeed.
Don't rush to gain something not there or that too shall soon perish like an unripe fruit snatched from its vine and cannot survive.
Know that time rules your life now until you are properly healed and only God's time will allow you to have what you need and not what you want.
You can rely on memories, yet do not dwell on the past or you'll find yourself trapped in yesterday's fears.
Always see the brighter things in life and your broken heart shall soon mend.*

A New Beginning

Starting over is hard to do; trying to forget the past knowing you can't.
Struggling for the future yet frightened of what it has to offer.
I hesitate but am eager to find out.
I think it's real, I feel it's right,
yet I can't rely on feelings alone for my emotions could alter at any time,
like riding a roller coaster not distinguishing which way I'm going next.
My new beginning makes me enjoy life and what it has to offer
and not be strained by the tribulations just as God makes me do.
His sweet spirit brightens my life as the sun does the earth on a dark gloomy day.
My new beginning only wants me happy, and I am, yet I still fear it may not last.
Wondering can I return his package
and give him more than his first and only love;
It's like taking one step forward contemplating falling two steps back.
We shouldn't look back, but our past is haunting our present.
Not wanting to let go, we are burdened,
horrified we'll forget our past and we won't.
Trying not to make the same mistakes,
we deny the truth of being able to fall in love again.
If we let nature take its course and allow God to control our lives, there will be no mistakes;
God will shelter us with His love so we may love like Him,
unconditionally, and nothing will ever come between us.
Now I see my new beginning as a brand new day
and I am anxious to find out what's to come.
I know my new beginning will bring pure joy and happiness,
and through God's will, he will be with me for eternity.

The Forgotten One

Deprived of happiness, depression is what I awaken to every morning.
Missing out on the joy of love, loneliness has become my mate.
Cupid must have passed me by, for my heart still yearns for his arrow.
Heart of glass shattered by the beatings of pain and heartache.
Nothing real to grasp, only dreams and fantasies I mistake for reality.
They are only false interpretations of a disturbed unconscious.
Giving my all yet receiving nothing in return;
Tired of fighting and trying to move on
only to be punctured by another devastating wound.
My body is weak, my soul is weary,
not knowing how much longer I can take this abuse.
Trapped in myself paying for crimes I never committed.
The more I try to escape, the worse my punishment is.
I can't satisfy the id of his mind.
No matter how much I give, it's not sufficient.
For every piece of me passed on to him and not replaced by his love,
a part of me deteriorates.
Soon I will have nothing to give, nor want to give;
to forget everyone as I have been forgotten.
People will only be by passers in my presence.
I shall never have the chance to give in return what I long to give;
for I am the forgotten one!

The Unknown

*Sometimes I sit, gazing into the realms of the unknown,
wondering what's really there.
I often wish I can go there,
yet I can only dream of what it is like.
Many are scared of the unknown,
yet I strive to seek the unknown.
The unknown is hope for the future.
It makes the present, past and the future, present.
The unknown sees what we are blind to,
and knows what we wish to know.
The unknown hears, talks, and does what we only desire,
for the unknown is everything!*

To Struggle

To struggle for what you want, means you have gained ambition;
Yet to strive for what you need,
Means you have reached success in life.
To have experienced what your heart yearns for means you have pursued love;
But to grieve over the unnecessary, means you have gained distress.
To achieve the impossible, means you have gained strength;
Yet to strive for only the best, means you have developed understanding.
Why want what you don't need? Why take what you don't want?
Neither is sufficient.

Deadly Stalker

Concealed as an intellectual yet impulsive being;
Luring every eye into his ruse.
Dismantling his victim as a predator to its prey.
The beginning is the end, the first is the last.
Your spirit is tormented, your soul left to die.
There is nowhere to run and nowhere to hide from this parasite;
For he has captivated your mind, body, and soul.
When his task is complete, knowing he'll succeed,
He vanishes . . . leaving you with nothing!

Wishing

Wishing you was close;
Wishing you was near.
Wanting to be close to you;
Wanting you to be here.

Missing you at night;
Missing you in the day.
Always wanting to talk to you;
With nothing much to say.

Waiting to touch your face again;
To have your lips compressed to mine.
To hold you and be in your arms;
To know everything will be fine . . .

Bewildered

Day to day I reminisce of what we have,
Wondering if it is real or can it last.
It's all new to me, and such a confusing state to be in;
Not knowing what to look for or expect.
I think of one thing, yet the opposite occurs,
I take the bad for good and good for bad.
I can't say what I feel or what I want to do,
For my conclusions are deterred.
I'm perturbed of what this could lead to,
Should I get out now or see things through?
I feel I'm stuck in the middle of two sides of a fence.
How is this possible? How did this commence?
The hows and whys I'll never know . . .
Shall I stay or will I go?

Misled

I thought it was different; I had to be misled.

He seemed to be unique; I must have misread.

The hour has struck; what was, is now gone.

What's done is done; we have to move on.

We went too far; our sunny days are wet.

Yet nothing has changed, since we first met.

Love at First Sight

From the moment our eyes met,
Our altered lives cohered.
Nothing could corrupt our spirits,
For the power of love was in control.
The twinkle in your eyes
Expressed the love in your heart.
Words were not needed, for our souls combined,
And our hearts became one.
In just one glance, we were bonded by the unknown . . .

For the Love of Her

Farewell my love, for I will no longer fight for nothing.
I hope she will satisfy you,
for I was put on this earth only to serve you, not control you.
Your happiness lies with her, and I can't change that.
If it is ever a time when you are not pleased, I'll be here;
Just reach for the stars, whisper to God, and I shall return.
Our times were good, but I guess not enough, her power over you is too strong.
Remember love endures, as I am love.
Your feelings for her selfishness will soon fade,
and you shall be free . . . to love . . . to love me.
Time awaits, and even though each minute feels like eternity,
when it is time for us to be joined again,
the time wasted will only be a few seconds, for infinity lies ahead.
Time will be of no consideration in love's eyes.
As long as feelings are shared, there is a chance for us.
If our feelings have changed, than this is goodbye . . .

Can't Let Go

It's the end of the road still I can't let go;
I'm confused inside and feeling kind of low.

He's nothing but a lying worthless jerk;
He does what he wants and doesn't care who hurts.

I want to let go of him so bad;
But I'm trapped in what I wish I had.

How can something so special be snatched away;
and haunt you for life day by day.

The innocence of life is out of control;
No more chivalry and love which God can unfold.

Every man for himself, the greed has moved on;
The selfishness will continue until love is gone.

I don't understand how I could love someone
who plays games with my mind as a way of fun.

He knows my mind inside and out;
and uses it against me without a doubt.

It's a shame the hell he put me through,
especially because we both know;

No matter how hard I try,
I don't think I'll ever be able to let him go.

Home

*Although you've left us here,
you're where you should be . . . home.
Away from the pain and misery of your old body and this world.
You can't even imagine the pain
and grief we feel down here,
but one day we will be with you again.*

Higher Ground

You left us here without a sound;
God has lifted you to a higher ground.
No more suffering and pain, for which we prayed for;
Sitting next to your Father, you weep no more.
We are missing you more and more each day;
We loved you so dearly in a special way.
Pleasing God daily and praying too;
That one day we may soon be with our Father and you.

Betrayed

I thought the love we shared was true;
Yet I was wrong, not again, him too?

My life was so full, vivid, and exciting;
But it was my best friend whom he was besiding.

Their relationship was so discrete and truly undercover;
No clues for me to follow, and all along they were lovers.

Then the secret was revealed, she, spilling her guts;
Everyone was upset; my heart was left in cuts.

My Heart Still Yearns

My heart still yearns for his love.
My soul bleeds for his spirit.
My body still longs for his touch.
My love has vanished never to return.
My mind is bewildered, for he never said goodbye.
I must face the end;
For I will never get the chance to be in his arms again.
I thought I could win his heart and touch his soul so he can be whole.
My dreams led me to a dead end destruction;
For his one and only love is himself,
And no one will ever change that.

So Smooth

So smooth with the tongue, so quick to deceive;
So easy to pretend, so capable of being believed.

Scandalous one with a plan of pure gold;
Caught me at a cheaper price, how could I have been so easily sold?

Star of the cast, yet written off the scene;
No chance to act, another will be weaned.

Extorted crown, yet queen for a day;
The minutes were memorable I have to say.

Yet onward I must go, another I shall meet;
You've played your game well, yet I am not another defeat!!!

Why?

Why are my eyes deceiving me? Him and her they cannot be.
Strolling down the midnight streets; as if a thief was lurking to creep.
I saw with my own tears; that all was lost to desolate fear.
It was all a dream forced into reality;
Maybe a nightmare I could really see.
Their destination I did not know;
Where they came from was not shown.
Yesterday was forgotten; for today was begotten.
Tomorrow was cut short, their plans had to abort;
All because my eyes watched them court.
No words were spoken of it on his part or mine;
All hope was lost for silence exposed his kind.
No reassurance or cover up proved the sight spoke the truth;
How can something explode so big yet be so minute?
Are my eyes really deceiving me?
Was there any more that I did not see?
I knew all was well and well was all;
Then why did the shock leave me appalled?
My stomach caved in like I was being stabbed;
A boxer pulverizing his opponent with more than jabs.
An unsettled soul, no love nor peace;
No earthly man to stand up for himself and make the crap cease.
Alone again in a world full of chaos with nothing to gain but a loss;
You play the field with Satan, you're bound to pay the cost . . .

FUTURE

Feeling the Unknown

Love is not a one way ticket,
It is not stamped for approval nor
Expired at another's expense . . .
Love endures.

Love is a feeling that can't
Be explained and often misused . . .
Love is a part of the unknown.

Love, a common bond shared between
Two people cannot fade;
Like a circle, it cannot break or open
Letting feelings drain out.

The feeling surrounds and embraces,
Fulfilling empty souls, magnetizing them to be one . . .
Love is unbelievable.

By love, two halves become a whole,
Two hearts become one;
Sharing feelings for eternity.

Revealing the unexpected and often desirable,
Luring the ambitious eager hearts,
Love is love . . .

My Sweet Love

*I stare into his puppy dog eyes
and dream of waking up in his arms every morning.
I feel the warmth of his smile
and tears start to slither down my face.
These tears are of joy and contentment he brings upon my life.
Oh what it would be like to have him forever.
His sweet spirit touches my soul in a way like no other
and brightens the deep dark bruised corners of my heart
so that I may be loved again.
God has crossed our paths for some profound reason
and I hope my sweet love stays for awhile.
I can't bear to not hear his voice, and laugh as he smiles;
and most of all, not to look into those eyes.
I am stunned in a trance by his eyes,
for they hold the key to his every secret thought.
For it is something about those eyes
that tell a story yet to be told.
His firmly shaped body arouses my emotions
to encounter his soft touch, so gentle, yet so real.
He gives the meaning to sweet in all aspects,
for his compassion is overwhelming, each deed a sweet dream.
I want my love to know that he'll always be a part of me,
even if God has us ordained to exit our perfect life.
My love for him will continue to grow whether far or near,
as of yesterday, today, and tomorrow . . .*

Dream Man

Heart of glass, smile of gold;
Understanding and sweet, setbacks will soon unfold.

The sun will shine, flowers will bloom;
Brightening someone's life, and being their groom.

Touch of softness, sensitive yet strong;
Happiness envelopes, one to him belong.

Funny enough to make any heart smile;
Love to sail a lifetime, along the river's Nile.

A fool would learn to weep;
If to him they did not keep.

Regret would bear upon one's back;
For it was in his eyes, a pure soul is his fact.

For each shattered corner of his heart replaced with steel;
Where God placed unconditional love and made those sore wounds heal.

And in turn giving that gift to one whose needs were sure;
To comfort one another, having faith that things will endure.

Mood of the Day

*I arise with a smile greeting the sun rays
Beaming through my window.
The morning awakens me with news of pleasantry ahead.
A few clouds in the sky will bring shadiness,
Yet nothing to dread for the darkness will not hinder my lighted path.
It's going to be a good day . . .*

Just To . . .

Just to see your smile, just to feel your touch;
Just to whisper I love you and say you mean so much.

Just to look into your eyes, to feel your soft brown skin;
Just to have your body next to mine, loving you can't be a sin.

Just to laugh at your jokes, just to cry when you feel pain;
Just to be by your side on sunny days and even when it rains.

Just to one day be your wife and maybe mother of two;
All in all I guess I'm saying how much I wish I could be with you . . .

Test of Time

*Our memories were strong enough to last a lifetime.
The honeymoon is over yet it is not the end;
This is beginning a new day and time.
You have gained more than a friendship
For something special was between us.
A force drove us together faster than two poles of a magnet.
Though we are taking separate paths we can cross whenever we like.
Our roads can be one if we believe.
The test of time determines the love and desire to be together.
Until we come together again,
I will keep you in the corner of my heart with a picture in my mind;
Waiting to see that smile of life upon your face.
I'll wish you goodnight,
Hoping you'll hear me as I tuck you in with my prayers and dreams.
I'll miss your laugh and sweet kisses goodnight,
Yet I know if I whisper to God,
You'll appear without a shadow of a doubt.
I will imagine your touch as you speak to my soul;
Feeling the warmth and sincerity of your heart.
God will compensate my weary spirit
And keep my heart as pure as gold so when our paths cross.
Nothing will intervene and drive us to separate directions.
Though the minutes will seem hours, and the hours, days;
Love can stand the test of time!!!*

I Laugh

They watch the stride in my step,
and the sway of my hips and I laugh.
They frown at my shoulder length hair blowing in the wind
and my caramel-colored skin that sparkles in the sunlight, and I laugh.
They chatter at the way they think I attract men with my luscious lips
and voluptuous body, when I know it is the twinkle in my eye,
my solemn smile and my sweet spirit, so I laugh.
They imitate my shape, my walk, and my attitude,
yet deep down inside they wish they could be me, so I laugh.
They envy my wisdom, charm and wit;
my status, my lifestyle, and of course my physique, and I laugh.
I laugh not because I know what is right,
but of what fools they make of themselves,
for the more attention they pay me, the taller I become.
Instead of knocking me down, they build me up,
and I laugh as I thank them . . .

Lips of Fire

Lips of fire, eyes of steel;
I am watched as I move step by step . . .
I'm gorgeous.

The arch in my step;
The dip in my back sways my cheeks from left to right . . .
I'm sexy.

The sweetness of my voice;
The slither of my tongue lures every man into my ruse . . .
I'm deadly.

The touch of my fingertips, so soft and warm;
Enables a man to melt in my hands . . .
I'm poisonous.

The use of my lips, the curve of my hips
Vanquishes all competition . . .
I'm sensuous.

The roundness of my breast
Or solemn smile is not mistaken for a weakness . . .
I am intelligent.

My voracious body is not surpassed by my wit;
For I am as wise as an owl and smarter than any man . . .
I'm powerful!

Opportunity Knocks

Not knowing what is going on inside that little heart;
I don't even know him, yet I feel I can't part.
Fantasizing of us together turning gray and old;
Sharing eternity through thick and thin, hot and cold.

Not sure if he's the right one, only time can unfold;
God's love will prevail, binding our hearts with gold.
I'm so confused; it's all happening so fast.
Is it just a game or will it last?

Am I blinded by the truth or is this opportunity knocking;
Is this a fantasy or reality, it's all too shocking.
All I can say is God's time will tell;
But as for my heart, it's singing all is well.

Lost Love

Sunshine has gone away yet a tear cannot be shed.
The deepest cut has not a frown though the pain is unspeakable.
Blind to the game yet feeling no defeat,
For the end has not yet come.
Nothing but remorse comes to the mind of the betrayed,
Knowing the culprit has only deceived himself.
For he has lost a precious stone, that very few possess,
Never to be found again.
Believing other stones were better, not one can compare.
The surface may not be desirable, yet the center is overwhelming . . .
if only it can be revealed!

How Can Life

How can life be so full, yet simultaneously empty?
Is he not who fulfills my desires? Is he not my dream come true?
When he's gone I'm half empty, when he's here I'm half full.
Day by day my cup becomes barren.
The more we are together, the more hollow I become.
Is he restoring my heart with nothingness as I pour out my love?
I want this to be more than physical, yet my mind and soul are dissatisfied.
My spirit is weary, my heart is sore.
The emptiness is overwhelmed by pain.
Tears can't even compensate my desolation . . . .

Three Falls

Three falls have passed, no words were said;
Wanting to capture your soul, and maybe be wed.

My heart is uncertain about why I'm so attached;
A plan was needed for you to be my catch.

A spider contemplating how to spin her web for you;
Bound to be stuck without a clue.

When I look into your eyes it's foggy to see;
What angle you are coming from, do you crave to be with me?

You are here in sight but not in soul;
Your mind is with others, I am muddled to your goal.

Do you imagine me day after day?
Or will neglect lead me astray?

I tuck you in at night with sweet dreams and prayers;
I store you in the center of my heart and show you I care.

I can give you my all and satisfy your every need;
I want to know your every thought,
To be there when you fail or succeed.

Just open up and let your heart be free;
Please discard your impedible wall and
Roam the world with me . . .

A Way Out

Why leave happiness for a fantasy?
True love lies within your heart yet not if your heart is deceived.
A rock may not be pleasing to the sight,
Yet what's in that rock is what counts the most.
Chasing false hopes and dreams will only lead to a dead end destruction.
Take things as they are and not what you perceive them to be,
And then little one, you can be freed from the chains of broken promises.
Your life has just begun, for you can love again if you let go of the past.
You have learned from this experience yet you don't owe anything.
There is no need to sacrifice yourself when there is only knowledge to gain.
God can set you free, precious one, if you open your eyes and soften your heart.
All it takes is a whisper to the sky and He shall lift all of your burdens.
You may reminisce of the past yet do not dwell in it,
For you will be trapped in yesterday's fears.
Aim high and you'll always reach the stars.
Remember, if it is meant to be, it will come again . . .

Shades of Black

*Whether I'm yellow, tan, coffee, mocha, chocolate or flat out
Black, I am subjected to injustice by non-colorist.
Whether I'm beautiful, funny, brilliant, reliable, or trustworthy,
I am labeled as "nothing" by those of non-color.
The colorless has even brainwashed us to divide amongst ourselves;
accepting those of the lighter shades,
making others of deep dark chocolate feel even more inferior.
They will stare at the glass ceiling pondering reaching the top.
Little do they know, they are only being used,
later to be thrown into the bottomless pit with the rest of us.
Don't they see that color brings life and meaning?
Without us of color, the world would not be what it is today.
We should be commended not ridiculed, cherished not abolished.
They say that we are not as smart,
as if the color of my skin really determines my brain capacity,
yet we added rhythms, soul, and feeling to everything we did,
making our discoveries so unique.
Though you kept us captive and stripped us of any identity,
we were smart enough to hold on to God,
and hope brought us to where we are today.
Our psalms spoke of our troubles, yet gave a promise for tomorrow.
Who would have ever thought tomorrow would be today?
We are all shades of black sent here by the Almighty One,
Blessed with life in order to fight the enemy, which is not human race.
Until we can see we are one, and not black and white,
the enemy will continue to divide and conquer
until you dislike even your sister, brother, father, or mother.*

Black is . . .

Black is beautiful, for there are many shades.
Black means strength, solid to the core.
Black means power, so absolute, non-erasable.
Black means fear, darkness unexposed.
But black seems to be evil, however, because of its unawareness.
To be aware is to know black, is to feel black, is to be black.
Variations of black vary weakness to strength.
The lighter shade has fear of darkness causing a known weakness.
Strength and fear are insurmountable
so the majority of lighter shade seems to overpower the darkness.
Yet through darkness there is always light that will cause an uproar.
So be buried no longer, be fooled no more, black is not a weakness.
Know that they are hand in hand;
There cannot be one without the other;
Where there is light there is dark and vice versa.
For we are all shades of one and one of many shades.

The Sun Still Shines

*Making yourself believe that the grass is green,
you fear reality will shatter your blind glass.
See things for what they are and not what you perceive them to be.
Reality will creep through the cracks exploding your heart into bits and pieces.
Yet through it all the sun still shines.
God will lift you up and carry you through, if you only believe.
Truth will give you eyes to see.
Faith will deliver, if you stay on bended knee.*

Friend?

His piercing smile, his dazzling eyes;
Caught my attention to my surprise.

For he didn't stand out nor brag or boast;
Yet it was near him where I was directed most.

He had a silly laugh and vanilla chiseled body;
He tickled my spirit; I had to get him close to me.

A subtle smile, kind words with my sweet voice;
I approached him right; I had to be his choice.

I gazed into his eyes and his into mine;
I made my mark, I'm first in line.

He had to be feeling what crossed my thoughts;
Our vibes were too strong, for we both were caught.

No public broadcasts just secret hellos;
For we have something that nobody knows.

Will it last? I don't know. Do I care? I'm not sure;
It seems to be a fling and I kind of want more.

His feelings are unknown, circumstances might prohibit,
I can't say where it will lead, I have to admit.

Our times were great and I will forget him not;
There's a place in my heart for you, friend, if that's all I've got . . .